HOW TO OVERACHIEVE W/O OVER COMMITTING

Quick Tips & Ideas for Getting Stuff Done at Work w/o Killing Yourself in the Process!

BRIAN HILLIARD

Table of Contents

Acknowledgements

I would first like to thank God for all of the blessings he's put into my life, which certainly includes the inspiration and people he's provided in my life so I could get this book done!

Second, I'd like to thank my brother Aaron, who has really been there for me over the years…lifting me up when I needed it, and providing the type support that has truly helped my life (and my business) get to where it is today.

And last, but certainly not least, I'd like to thank my partner Deb, who has inspired me to new levels in my life, my business and in our relationship. She has helped me find and rediscover various aspects of who I am as a person, and I can say with absolute certainty that I couldn't have gotten to where I am today without her support.

Thank you.

<u>Introduction</u>

If you've somehow found yourself reading this book, then chances are you're an Overachiever.

People might describe you as a hard working, diligent person who they trust to get things done. On the job, some might even describe you as "a real go getter" – the type who takes on additional responsibility, while still moving their projects forward.

And while all of this sounds great, there's just one problem.

As you take on more and more work, and accept more responsibility – both at the job and within the community – you can sometimes find yourself over committed. In other words, your life is so filled with projects, deadlines and countless meetings, that at times you feel like there's too much going on. You're being pulled in too many different directions.

And that's frustrating too, since you consider yourself the type who does what they say they're going to do, but sometimes you simply don't have the time.

So you stay late, work through lunch and maybe even bring some work home, but it still isn't enough. There just aren't enough hours in the day.

Fortunately though, this isn't entirely your fault. As a matter of fact, it's something I call the Achiever's Burden, and the typical characteristics are as follows:

- Hard worker.
- Likes being busy.
- Likes the feeling of accomplishing their goals.

- Wants to do things themselves.
- Doesn't like to delegate.
- Likes to finish what they started.
- Gets very absorbed in a task.
- Internally motivated to "make a difference" in their work.

Most of the time this behavioral set is considered a strength, and as a result makes you a desirable person on the job. However, those same characteristics can also lead to that person over committing themselves as they try to get all of the work done.

My book on How to Overachieve without Over Committing can help by showing you how to deal with the tons of responsibilities you have, without killing yourself in the process.

I'll show you how to strike the balance between being a hard worker, and not letting the job take over your life. Between being more productive, and constantly staying busy. In a nutshell, you'll learn how to excel on the job and at home, and get the work/life balance you deserve.

Because let's face it, whether you're a Leader, Organizational Professional or Business Owner, you can't keep up this break-neck pace forever.

And who needs it?

The sleepless nights. The excessive hours at work. The time away from your friends and family. Unless of course you like waking up at 3:00 in the morning, unable to get back to sleep because of all the work you've got to do.

(If that's the case, then slowly put this book down and step away from the counter.)

But if you're interested in a real change in the quality of your life, then I can show you some easy ways to make that happen.

Each of our tips is a simple, yet powerful tool representing the collective wisdom of other business professionals, as well as our own experience. You'll also notice that while each tip is a "free-standing" technique, collectively they create a solid foundation to be used in any situation.

In a nutshell, How to Overachieve without Over Committing is perfect for "go getters" looking to get a little sanity back in their lives.

And who couldn't use a little more of that?

All the best,

Brian

CHAPTER 1

<u>The Secret for Overachieving without Over Committing</u>

Want the secret for learning how to overachieve without over-committing?

Recognize that you're NOT going to get everything done.

Now I know that can be hard for some people and please don't take it personally, because it's not meant to be a knock on your ability to get stuff done.

It's simply the harsh reality that all successful people face, which is the amount of time and energy we have as human beings, is dwarfed by the level of activities that we as high achievers want to accomplish.

Simple as that.

You might be thinking "Okay, so if that's the secret, then what do I do to move forward and be more productive?"

Easy.

Number 1, you need to differentiate the "high impact" activities in your work day from everything else.

And Number 2, you need to prioritize your day so that two or three of these "highly impactful" activities get done regularly.

Sounds easy enough, right?

Well, here's the catch…

As high achievers, we LOVE crossing things off our "to-do" list. Meaning, the more items we can cross off during a particular day, the more we feel like we're being productive.

But here's the thing, in most cases, those "easy to cross off things" are NOT very impactful to our overall professional success.

This is why you can spend the entire day running around feeling busy (and getting stuff done), yet at the end of the day, you realize that you haven't actually accomplished anything of real importance.

And again, it's not because you were just sitting around doing nothing.

It's because the things you did do – answering emails, commenting on social media, putting out fires – while feeling productive at the time, weren't necessarily the most impactful things you could have done to move closer towards your stated work goals.

You might be thinking "Alright, give me an example of how doing less actually moves me forward faster (This ought to be good.)"

Not a problem.

As an example, let's say there are 30 things in the total work universe that you need to get done for that particular week. (For a LOT of people reading, having only 30 things to do during a week would be considered a vacation, but for the sake of discussion let's just go with it.)

Now the old way is to just jump head first into that list, and run and move as fast as you can to try and cross off as much stuff as possible so that by the end of the week you've got all 30 things done.

Except that doesn't happen, does it?

Because while you're busy trying to do those 30 things, 5 more come at you every day, so by the time Friday rolls around, you simply didn't have enough time and energy to get it all done.

That's the "old way."

Instead, what if we take a different approach?

So we still have the 30 things on our list for the week, but instead of the old head-long "get it all done even though we know that's not going to happen" approach, what if we say instead, "All right, well what are the most impactful 10 or 15 things that we know are going to have a huge impact on our work life?"

And then made it a point to put 1 or 2 of THOSE things on our to-do list every day, and obviously make it a priority to move forward in those areas.

So as an entrepreneur, these might be things that allow us to generate more paying clients. Examples include:

- Attending a networking event,
- Making calls for potential speaking engagements,
- Creating proposals.

As an organizational professional, these might be things that your manager is asking you for or things that are going to move you closer to getting a promotion or a better/different job down the line. Examples include:

- Engaging in some form of higher education (master's or doctoral degree),

- Coming in an hour early, closing the door, and knocking out a project or two for the Boss,
- Actively developing relationships with others in your organization.

Or as a business leader, these might be the kinds of things that move your team forward and allows the organization to excel. Examples include:

- Coming in an hour early, closing the door, and knocking out a project or two that will have a positive, exponential effect on the team,
- Taking a Leadership class or attending a Conference,
- Spending some "quality time" with various team members to better understand what THEY want in their professional life…and how you as the leader can best facilitate.

Regardless, we've prioritized 15 things from the original 30 that we're now going to tackle, based on the impact that we KNOW it's going to provide at the end of the day.

And what kind of effect do you think that's going to have in your day-to-day life?

Well for one, you'll probably feel a sense of accomplishment because you'll be getting highly impactful stuff done, rather than just playing a giant game of "Whack-a-Mole" throughout your day.

Number two, you'll probably feel a lot less stressed because again, you're not running around all day trying to keep a bunch of balls in the air. Why?

Because you've already acknowledged that some things won't get done, therefore the sheer volume of balls that you feel like you need to keep up with will be reduced.

Number three and this is my personal favorite: You'll experience more success at work!

How can I be so sure about that? Because the things you are spending your time and energy on are directly related to the things that you've already determined are going to have a high impact on your professional success.

So going back to our earlier examples.

Maybe you're an entrepreneur who's looking to get more paying clients as I mentioned before. Well, I wonder what happens if you start focusing on getting more speaking engagements or meeting more people through networking, or increasing your social media presence? You'll probably get more paying clients!

Or maybe you're a business leader and you're looking to get a little more production from your team. Well, I wonder what would happen if you as the leader spent more time with the individuals on your team – really got a chance to better understand what THEY want out of their work experience – and see how you as their manager could point them in that direction?

I'm guessing they would feel more loyalty, be more productive and (wait for it), get more stuff done as a TEAM!

I think you're starting to get the idea.

> You see the secret for overachieving without over-committing isn't trying to come up with a super-efficient way to get through all 30 things on your list during a particular week.

The secret is cutting that list in half by prioritizing, and then being super focused on getting that stuff done regularly because generally speaking, moving forward in those high-impact areas will have a HUGE impact on your overall success.

Now, I understand that this is going to be a shift for a lot of people and you still might be a little incredulous even while you're still reading this.

But don't take my word for it, try it out for the next week.

In other words, take a look at all the things that you need to do during a 5-day work week or whatever and focus on the things that are going to drive you as an organizational professional and/or leader forward.

And write those things down as items that you're going to tackle that particular week. Then from there, daily, you're going to want to take two or three, or four items from that overall list and put that on your to-do list for that day. And last but not least, make it a point to spend at least an hour or two a day in one of those three areas.

Believe me, you'll see a world of difference!

CHAPTER 2

Manage Your Energy...Not Your Time

One of the things I talk about a lot when it comes to overachieving without over-committing is the idea of managing your energy...not your time.

> And the reason it's super important is that most people think success is a conversation around managing your time so that you can tackle tasks most efficiently and obviously get things done.
> I think what's changed in the past 20+ years is the sheer volume of options and things we can do with our time.

Or to put it another way, overachieving without over-committing is LESS of a conversation around efficiency and productivity, and more a discussion around marshaling the finite level of energy you have daily, and intentionally directing that towards high-impact areas that you KNOW will facilitate more success at work.

But before we jump into how to do this exactly, let's first cover a couple of key principles for success.

Principle 1: All tasks are NOT created equally.

Again, this is something you've heard me talk about a LOT and it's crucial for making this concept work. So as a quick recap, "all tasks are not created equally" simply means that there are some things that will give you a bigger bang for your buck than others.

This goes back to the 80/20 Rule we talked about earlier (Chapter 2) and gets at something I like to call ROE. So in business, you've heard of Return on Investment (ROI) I'm sure. Well, this is EXACTLY the same, except it's a Return on Energy. (I thought of that myself. ☺)

So as an example, one of the things my girlfriend and I talk about is keeping the house clean. Cleaning the kitchen, cleaning the laundry area, cleaning the living room, cleaning our bedroom, cleaning my office…you get the idea.

And while I have zero problems with that, if you don't watch out, you can spend ALL of your time and energy vacuuming floors, folding laundry, and emptying the dishwasher. Again, not a problem because that's part of having a house, but at some point, you have to decide, "Is spending more time cleaning up the kitchen – right now – going to get me to where I want to go in my personal and/or professional life?"

Now sometimes the answer is yes.

My girlfriend likes the kitchen clean, and most of the time, if it's dirty or dishes are all over the place, I'll take a few minutes during the day to clean it up real quick.

But other times, the answer is no. Yes, I would like to have a clean kitchen, but I don't have the energy right now to put those dishes into the dishwasher, mop up the floor AND get ready for my presentation coming up next week.

So I choose "getting ready for a presentation" or "recording a podcast" right then so that my business can move forward and I'll get back to the kitchen another time. Or to put it more bluntly: Recognizing that I have a finite amount of energy, I chose to spend it on an area that would move my business forward versus something else (in this case cleaning the kitchen, but it could have just as easily been "working out").

And that's just one example.

Another one would involve email.

Does spending another 20 mins "catching up" on email help me move my team forward as a leader, or would I be better off knocking out a quick project or even just walking over to someone's desk and having a good conversation?

You see the difference?

Just remember, all of us have a finite amount of energy every day, and where you direct and use that energy at work will play a LARGE part in your overall success.

Principle 2: We live in a hyperactivity-oriented world, meaning that the "natural" course of things is always going to be to do more and go faster and get stuff done!

And while that's fine, I encourage you to remember that rest and recuperation are VERY much a good thing to do during that process, otherwise, you'll literally break down.

I learned this lesson back in 2002 when I first started my business. I was laying on the couch not doing anything because I was sick…again.

And when I say "sick" I mean, not moving…feeling dizzy…on the couch for a week kind of thing. And this was the 2nd time it had happened in 18 months.

And it wasn't until the 3rd time the following year that I finally learned this lesson: "Brian, you can't go go go ALL the time without taking a break. You have to incorporate an element of rest into your day/week/month/year, otherwise, you're going to have this keep happening to you every 7 months."

> And it was right then and there I realized that I had a choice: I could incorporate rest and recuperation into my daily routine or my body could do it for me.

I chose Door #1 and would highly recommend you do the same.

And just to be clear, I'm not trying to take away your achievement or your action or your go-gettedness...I'm trying to give you some balance.

I'm trying to reconcile this action oriented, "go, go, go" approach that a lot of us have, and instead incorporate more of an energy orientation, where you recognize that you only have a certain amount each day and there needs to be a balance between "rest" and "action".

And when you bring those two points together, what you get is a situation where you can get stuff done without killing yourself in the process. Because you're focused on movement AND rest as a matter of course.

So with all of that said, let's get into some actual tactics that you can use more to intentionally manage your energy throughout an otherwise hectic work day.

5-Step Roadmap for Managing Your Energy...Not Your Time

Step 1: Download Your Mind.

Let's face it, for most people, we have a LOT on our minds!

There's stuff we need to do at work, calls to make, emails to answer, and for leaders...team members to engage and grow. And of course, that's not getting into the day-to-day stuff at home (for me, cooking dinner and making sure I take some time off in the evening!).

But here's the thing: Keeping up with all of that stuff takes up a tremendous amount of energy in the background. And this is energy that for the most part, people don't even realize they're expending.

I tell people it's like having a bunch of programs running in the background on a computer, and while any one thing might not be a lot, all of it together is causing the computer – and in this case you – to slow down. So what can you do to "download your mind?"

Start by spending 20 minutes with a piece of legal size paper and write EVERYTHING you need to do as it pertains to your work life down. Things like, "write a proposal," "answer email," "meet with the Team," and "talk to my Manager about X"…put it all down on a sheet of paper.

Then go buy yourself a whiteboard and hang it up in your office (if you work from home) or get a smaller one if you have a desk at a physical location and put it up there.

Then transfer everything from that list to the whiteboard.

> And now you have everything OUT of your mind and in a place you can trust. That in and of itself will have a HUGE impact on your energy levels, because like I said earlier, I had no idea how much energy I was spending trying to keep track of stuff that I didn't want to forget.

But ever since I implemented this technique myself, I found my overall energy to uptick dramatically.

Step 2: Determine what it is that you want exactly.

Now, this is tricky for a lot of people, because most people know more about what they DON'T want than what they do. And part of the problem with living and working in a hyperactivity-oriented world is that they don't take the time to figure out where the finish line is exactly, so they just keep going and going and pushing and going…until they burnout

We don't want that.

So let's take a look at what YOU want exactly. What's the point of all of this work and time you're putting into the office?

For me, we want to retire in a place like Spain or Portugal or someplace like that.

And we want to do it in the next 5 years.

So as I'm sure you can imagine, that provides a ton of clarity and does wonders for helping me focus my energy (and usually my time), on work-related items that will help me reach that goal.

So my question is, what do you want exactly?

As a leader, what do you want from yourself and your team?

As an organizational professional, what do you want from yourself and your career?

As a business owner, how do you want to show up in others' lives?

These are all good questions that will help you move in the right direction, and provide some clarity for why you're doing what you do.

Step 3: Create a plausible stretch goal.

This is super important because this will now give you something to shoot for and reach. Using myself as an example, I have a goal as to how many new clients I want to pick up over an 8 week period.

Not only does that keep me focused on talking to new people, but it also helps me not to rest on my laurels and get too comfortable with the revenue I currently have.

For you, it might be different.

I mentioned our desire to get to Portugal earlier, so that might be something you're looking at, or maybe you have something more immediate.

No problem.

The key is that it needs to be both a "stretch" goal…something that you can't easily reach and therefore would be very satisfying when you do get there.

As well as a "plausible" one…something that you can absolutely environing happening, even if you don't know how to do it right now.

And it's that last part I want to talk about because a lot of times, you hear about these huge stretch goals (I want to earn a \$1M next month!), but if you don't believe them or they don't seem plausible to you…then the likelihood of success, in my opinion, is considerably lower, regardless of the number of daily affirmations you make!

But when you create a goal that is a "stretch," something that is further out than you would normally go. But not soo far out in the stratosphere that you can barely comprehend it (therefore plausible), I think you'll find yourself to be a LOT more successful.

Step 4: Implement a morning routine.

This is simultaneously one of the easiest and hardest for us overachievers to do because on one hand, you don't necessarily have to do anything new (easy), but you have to find the time to create a repeatable, calming process first thing in the morning (a little hard at first).

Alright, now let's first clear up a common misconception when I talk about this, which is the idea that a morning routine has to involve 7 hours of yoga and a 1 ½ mile run.

It doesn't!

Personally, my morning routine ranges from 5 minutes to 60, just depending on what my day looks like and when I get up. Here's what I normally do:

- Get up and pet Luna (one of our cats). She ALWAYS wants to have a conversation around petting and purring first thing in the morning, and I used to rush this until I realized how soothing it was for me. ☺
- Second, go to the bathroom, put on my shoes and go for a 15 min walk outside. I got this from Ben Greenfield, where he says that if you want to increase your body's metabolism, going on a walk first thing was a great fat-burning exercise.
- After that, use my foam roller. This helps me stay flexible and wakes up my body after my walk.
- Once I'm back in the house, jump into some Scripture. I have an app on my phone (Olive Tree Bible) which provides different reading plans in the Bible and I'm usually in the middle of one, so I read whatever passage is presented that day.
- And last but not least, do some meditation.

Now if I don't have a ton of time in the morning for whatever reason, then I scale that down. But if I have the full hour, then I'll do ALL of that.

But figure out what works for you.

I know some of you guys have kids that you need to get up for school so a 60 min routinue might not be feasible, and that's perfectly fine. Just make sure the first 30 minutes of your day are NOT dominated by running around doing a bunch of stuff for everyone else, and instead, focus on getting you off to a good, calming start to your day.

Step 5: Initiate an evening cool down.

Out of all the things we've talked about, this is probably one of the most important, because it allows you to disperse all of the chaotic, sometimes negative energy that you picked up throughout the day, and instead, calm your mind and your thoughts. Now it doesn't have to be this huge deal, but there does need to be a degree of intentionality to this, otherwise, you won't get a good night's sleep and you won't feel refreshed when you wake up.

Oh, and the evening cool-down is a lot more flexible than the morning routine, so there's that. ☺ Anyway, here's what I do:

- First off, I make sure to give myself a specific time that I want to go to bed. For me, it's 9:15 pm...for you, it might be later, which is fine. But have a definite time you want to go to bed.

- Second, I don't watch any high-intensity movies or action thrillers before I go to bed. I also make it a point not to get into heavy conversations with my partner.

- Third, I'll sometimes read a magazine (e.g., Eating Well) or engage in a hobby or even watch a little light movie on NetFlix or something.

- And fourth, if I've had a particularly hard day, I'll do another meditation about 15 minutes before going to bed.

If you find yourself having trouble getting to sleep (or staying asleep), I'd highly recommend an evening routine similar to this. My girlfriend will sometimes take a bath after a particularly challenging day, so feel free to find what works for you.

> But regardless, managing your energy not your time is a conversation around incorporating those high levels of activity with some level of rest and recuperation – what I like to call "downtime" – so you're not so exhausted and depleted at the end of the day, and you actually have a life at home AND at work you enjoy!

CHAPTER 3

<u>The 1 Rule That Helped Me "Level Up" my Production & Dial Down my Stress</u>

Want to know the one rule that has been an absolute lifesaver for me?

The 80/20 Rule.

Now I'm sure you've heard of this before, but if you haven't, it simply says that 80% of your results are going to come from 20% of your efforts. It was invented by an Italian economist named Pareto in the late 1800s when he discovered that 80% of the wealth in Italy was obtained by 20% of the people.

At that time, that was super counterintuitive and some people were having a hard time believing it, so he went a step further and did some additional research to see if that rule held true in other areas.

And it did!

Turns out this 80/20 rule was true in farming as well.

In other words, 80% of the food and produce grown in Italy at the time was produced by only 20% of the farmers. So after doing even more research and finding even more examples where this was true, he coined the "Pareto Principle" which said that in most cases, 80% of your results – whether it's wealth, farming, or success at work – are going to come from 20% of your resources, which is terrific news for overachievers!

Why?

> Because that means as overachievers, we don't have to do everything on our list to be a success!

So let's say you're an organizational professional. According to the 80/20 rule, if I were to come in and take a look at your to-do list today, it's highly likely that I could find 3 or 4 things that if you could make solid headway on throughout the week, you would absolutely accelerate your success and be MUCH closer to your goals at work.

Again, just by doing thes 3 or 4 things, versus say the other 7 or 8 things on that same list, you're going to be further along.

And that's NOT to say that those other things are unimportant or shouldn't be done. I'm just saying that those 3 or 4 – if you could get them done during the week – would have a HUGE impact on your professional success.

Which as I also said is GREAT news for us overachievers, because it debunks the idea that we have to run around like a crazy man trying to get everything done. Turns out, in theory at least, we only have to do the things the 20% of the things on our list that will yield 80% of the results.

Now while that sounds great in theory, how can we make that a reality in practice when you've got a 1,001 things going on and people are coming up to you all the time?

Great question and let me share with you the 1 thing that has REALLY helped me out in that regard.

My calendar.

That's right. When I started using my calendar to schedule time into my day to execute these high-impact activities (the ones that will give me 80%

of my results), I absolutely "leveled up" my production, while dialing down my stress. ☺

Let me first provide a little background and then I can walk you through a real-life example.

So as a coach and speaker, one of the challenges that I still run into today is being able to balance my coaching activities with my paid speaking engagements.

In other words, to get paid to speak, you need to let others know that you even exist. Which means making calls, sending emails, and identifying groups that bring in paid speakers.

And all of that is fine…but it also takes time (even with the help of my virtual assistant). ☺

And on top of that: Paid speaking is NOT an immediate revenue generator.

This means that the conferences and events that I do wind up booking are in most cases 3, 6, and even 12 months down the road. And this can be a challenge, because today, right now…the mortgage doesn't pay for itself!

That's where the coaching comes in because getting a coaching client not only takes less time, but the "payoff" is a lot shorter. I can get 2 to 4 thousand dollars on average within 3 weeks with a coaching client, versus getting that same amount 6 months down the road with a paid speaking engagement.

(Sidebar: Sometimes people ask, "So why do speaking at all then? Just stick with the coaching?" And the answer is that the 2 to 3 grand is just from the speaking event itself. That doesn't count the additional coaching and consulting clients you'll get FROM the audience members, which if I play my cards right, could turn into a total revenue figure of over $10,000 per speaking event. That's why I do it. ☺)

Anyway, the point is that my success on the coaching side is able to more quickly translate into bottom-line revenue in the form of a paying coaching client, then that same level of success from a paid speaking engagement simply because it's going to happen at a faster rate.

So if I find myself facing a typical 8 hours per day, I have to make a decision: dedicate the time that will help me get a paying coaching client within the next couple of weeks or dedicate the time that will help me get 3 to 4 times that amount in 6 to 12 months?

And for a LONG time, my choice was to try and do both.

> But here's what happened. Even though I said I wanted both, I didn't prioritize the paid speaking aspect of my business enough.

In other words, I would work really hard on the coaching side and hope that I could find the time to move the paid speaking part forward. And as anyone who's ever tried that "strategy" before, you know how it worked out: the paid speaking activities just kept falling through the cracks when it comes to my regular week-to-week activities.

I never find the time to work on the "high impact" area of my business, even though it was worth 3 to 4 times the total revenue.

So what did I do when I realized this was happening?

I scheduled the time into my calendar just like I would a meeting.

So 3 days a week I usually schedule between the hours of 8 and 10:00 a.m. something that I call "paid speaking" activities. And as the name implies, these are the times on Tuesday, Wednesday, and Thursday when I'm making calls, sending emails, and going through some of the different websites and lead generators I have set up.

I'll also use it to work on presentations for an upcoming event, like the slides or something along those lines. But the point is that generally speaking, for two to three hours a day, again 2 to 3 days a week, I make it a point to be executing activities that will generate paid speaking engagements.

And you want to know a funny thing that happened on my way to better prioritizing my paid speaking business? My coaching AND my paid speaking picked up!

> That's right. By getting more organized with how I spent my time and making that high-impact area more of a priority by putting it into my calendar, I generated more success than previously realized.

Now with all of that said, how does that translate to what you're doing as a leader, organizational professional, or business owner? Easy.

Step 1: Identify the activities that you believe will drive 80% of your results.

Don't get caught up in what's "realistic" or not, or what you currently have time for. Just identify the 3 or 4 items on your list right now, where if you made significant headway on them this week, your professional life would be a LOT better off the following week and/or month.

So as an example, let's say as a business leader, I want the team to increase production by say 15 to 20% by the end of next quarter.

And let's also say that the main driver behind getting that result is updating the systems and processes the team uses on a day-to-day basis. So as the leader of that group, I've taken it upon myself to:

- Create better job descriptions, so it's more clear what my expectations are for each position,
- Develop some written processes so that everyone is on the same page on HOW to be successful in a particular job, as well as some documentation that will help others backfill that position when the original person is out of the office for whatever reason.

And there might be some other things I work on personally as well to move that goal forward, but I think you get the idea.

Now if you've ever been in a situation where you've had to do that, even for a "small" 10-person team, you know that a 15 to 20% increase in production is totally feasible.

But you also know that this process is not something that you can do overnight, nor will it have an immediate payoff.

So what can you do as a leader in that situation when you recognize that there's a project out there that will drive 80% of your results as it relates to increasing team production, yet you're constantly barraged by all of the other things on a day-to-day basis?

Step 2: Schedule time into your calendar to work on that project.

So if it were me, I'd recommend 2 to 3 times a week for maybe 60 to 90 minutes where I will personally handle things in that regard.

Maybe some of that time I'm going in and identifying what I'd like the systems and processes to look like in a perfect world. Maybe I even use some of that time to talk to some of the individuals on the team just to make sure that I've got my ducks in a row in terms of what they do on a day-to-day basis.

Heck, maybe I'm even spending some of that time talking to my manager to let him/her know what I'm doing and pave the way for us to move forward (e.g., talking to the IT people so we can easily implement the changes).

But the point is that I've scheduled time into my calendar, just like a meeting, taking care of that business!

Step 3: Make some adjustments.

This is especially true if it's the first time you're using the calendar in this way, or if it's a big project that you haven't done before.

Maybe Tuesday, Wednesday & Thursday for your "meeting" times aren't the right days.

Or maybe mornings are better than afternoons since that will allow you to get your high-impact work done when fewer people are in the office. (I do that myself as I got up at 5:30 am to start the process of writing this chapter for today.)

Or maybe you wanted 3 days a week, but you can only do 2 days and that's fine too. But regardless, you're going to have to make some adjustments, and don't panic or give up because "it's not working" as immediately as you thought.

Here's the bottom line: The 80/20 Rule absolutely works.

It works in economics, it works in farming, it's worked for me …and it will work for you as a leader, business owner, or organizational professional as well.

So go back and review those 3 steps real quick and get that into action starting THIS week…and let's see how much of an impact this can have for you.

CHAPTER 4

<u>4 Words that Have Helped Me Get Stuff Done!</u>

Are you ready for the 4 words that have REALLY helped me over the years: **FINISH WHAT YOU STARTED.**

Not only have they allowed me to be more successful in terms of getting stuff done, but they've also allowed me to do it in a way that's less stressful and less overwhelming in general.

And even though the words are very straightforward, let's unpack them a little bit so you can see EXACTLY how I implemented this concept into my life, because let's face it: As an overachiever, and I think I can speak for most of us, I had (have) a lot on my plate.

Which in itself isn't necessarily a bad thing, except for one little problem…

> I have a habit of trying to work on ALL of those things at once.

In other words, I might have 15 items on my to-do list for a particular day, and because I wanted to do "everything," what I'd do is work on Item 1 for 40 mins. Then remember something I need to do for Item 3 and work on that for 20 mins. Then try and get back to Item 1…only to be interrupted by something/someone relating to Item 7 on the list.

And then I'd still have to circle back to Item 3 (no wait! Item 1 first THEN 3), and by the time it was all said and done: It was 2 pm, I hadn't eaten lunch AND I hadn't actually completed one thing!

And if you've ever found yourself in that situation you already know this to be true: It's frustrating, stressful, and discouraging all at once!

Because you're thinking to yourself, I've been so busy the entire day, but don't have anything to show for it!

And the main reason I did this was the mistaken belief that by keeping all the balls up in the air I was moving forward.

Again, incorrect.

Instead what happened was I ended up NOT moving forward as quickly in ANY of those areas, because instead of focusing 40 mins on Item 3 and getting that done, I dispersed my time, energy, and thought process over too many areas, which greatly inhibited my ability to be successfully complete any of those projects.

Darren Hardy talked about this during one of his productivity courses and the term is "switching." As in, by me switching from one project to the next, to the next, to the next, and back to the first, I made the road longer to travel because I kept having to regain my thought process as a result of switching gears.

Which meant that instead of feeling good about myself about a job well done, I felt exhausted, depleted and a little frustrated, because even though I was super busy for eight or nine hours, there wasn't anything that I could put my finger on as what I accomplished that day.

Sound familiar?

But when I picked up the mantle of "finish what I started"…OMG, my life get so much better!

So as an example, let's take a look at what that looks like in an organizational setting, where you might be the leader of a team, because you REALLY have a lot of stuff coming at you and trying to pull you in different directions, and worse than that, it might not feel like things you can control.

So at one point you've got your manager coming up and asking for stuff.

At another point, you've team members that you need to work with and/or show some leadership with.

Oh…and you've got your own 15-point "to-do" list of things that need to get done that day, so yeah…you've got a lot going on.

So in that setting, how do you finish what you started when it seems like everyone is coming at you from all different directions?

Well there is no silver bullet answer, and in today's modern workforce there's going to be a degree of managing multiple priorities, so reading this book won't make THAT go away unfortunately.

But there are some ways to be successful, without it having such a detrimental impact on your overall health and well-being.

Recommendation #1: Knock off some of that high-priority, high-impact work early on in the day.

Now I've mentioned this before, how as a business owner, I get my day started super early at 7:00 a.m. Now with that said, I know that's not for everyone either in terms of being an early bird or needing to get the kids out of the house.

Totally get that.

But even if you can work something out on the home front where you can get into the office early once or twice a week so you can work on those highly impactful projects, you are going to see a real lift in terms of your productivity (you'll be getting stuff done while no one is in the office to bother you) and fulfillment (you'll feel better about yourself once the day gets started because you will have accomplished something)!

Again, I understand that this might not be for everyone, but this has allowed me to get in solid hours worth of uninterrupted work moving forward - usually in an area that has a high impact relating to my overall success (see 80/20 rule) - and that has helped when it comes to the overall outlook I have at the end of the day.

Recommendation #2: Consider breaking down your projects into manageable bite-size pieces.

I got this from the book "Getting Things Done: The Art of Stress-free Productivity" by David Allen and it's been a real lifesaver.

So one of the examples I gave earlier was a leader who was trying to increase the production of their team by 15 to 20% by the end of the quarter. And as you might remember, she realized in order to do that, there was going to be an update in some of the systems and processes that the team regularly engaged with.

And again, for anybody who's gone down this road of updating systems, processes, and operations manuals, you already know how much of a bear that project can be.

Now the old way would be writing "work on updating team systems" on your to-do list. And while that reminds you what to work on, it doesn't give you the sense of accomplishment at the end of the day, because you could literally spend 2 hours working in that area and still not be halfway through the project.

Meaning you would still have that item on your to-do list and it has the potential to feel like you didn't make any forward progress that day.

However the new way – again from Mr. Allen's book – is to break that project down into some manageable bite-size pieces and put THEM on your to-do list for the day.

So your list might look like this.

Work on Updating Team Systems & Processes

- *Talk to 3 team members to see what their current process is for onboarding a new client.*
- *From those same 3 members, gather any recommendations THEY might have to make it better.*
- *Talk to IT and see if what they want (the Team members) is possible.*

You see how that is still under the auspicious of "updating the systems and processes," while at the same time, giving you some concrete to-do items that you can easily work on and then cross off when completed at the end of the day.

Here's another example.

Let's say you're a leader and you want to update the job descriptions of all the members of your team. You're NOT looking to fire anyone, but maybe we could combine some things or swap things around with certain people, and maybe THAT would be good enough for a 10% uptick in productivity.

No problem. Your first few items might be:

- *Review the job descriptions of the 3 people on my Team.*
- *Talk to them and see if they think it's accurate or if they are doing some things that aren't listed in the current manual.*
- *Ask them if they wanted to take on any additional responsibility, for example, in other areas along the process, as a way of enhancing their resume.*

Again, very concrete. Very straightforward.

And VERY easy to "finish what you started" and feel good about your work output at the end of the day.

Recommendation #3: Buy yourself a 6-pack of Jr. Legal Size paper ($4 at Wal-Mart) and have one on your desk at ALL times, that way if you get interrupted in the middle of a task you can just jot down real quick.

Now that might seem like an odd one under the heading of "finish what you started," but the reason I put this in there is that the reality of the modern workday is that you're going to get interrupted a LOT. And while we want to do things to avoid that from happening, this falls under the category of mitigating its effect on you to "finish what you started" AFTER you get interrupted…which is why I recommend the following process when you're in the process of getting interrupted.

1. Ask the person to wait one second.
2. Pull out the Jr legal pad and jot down real quick what your next step is on the project you're currently working on, that way you can capture your current train of thought.
3. Turn your attention to the person who interrupted you and ask what you can do for them.

"Brian…how is THAT going to help me reduce the impact of interruptions and be more successful at finishing what I started?"

Great question.

And the answer goes back to those "switching costs" that I mentioned earlier with Darren Hardy. It takes us a good 3 to 5 minutes to regain our train of thought when it comes to restarting a project after we get interrupted.

And the reason is that it takes that amount of time for us to regain our thinking and obviously get back on track.

However, if you write it down real quick (e.g., "pull XYZ file from the ABC folder when I get back"), you'll find that it's MUCH easier to jump right back into the flow and MUCH faster than if you hadn't done anything.

Believe me, I do this myself (although not as much as I probably should), and I ALWAYS notice the difference.

So for me as a business owner, a good example is when I'm putting together a proposal for a potential new client.

Meaning I'm working on this document, which usually takes about 30 to 40 minutes, and the phone rings or someone walks into my office with an issue I need to address right away. Instead of just dropping everything and putting it down, what I try to do on most occasions is write real quick on a junior legal pad like two or three notes as to what I was thinking or points that I wanted to make on the proposal.

That way when I do come back I don't have to spend 10 more minutes trying to re-pick up my train of thought.

Believe me, this sounds like a small thing, but in the absence of being able to finish what you started straight through, this will help you pick up your train of thought faster, so you can get to the finish line with your project with less "switching" time.

Recommendation #4: And this is one that I am still struggling with myself, but maybe you guys can do better at it than me: Keep the open tabs on your browser to a minimum. ☹

Now like I said earlier, this is an area I'm still struggling with. Meaning that if you were to go to my computer right now you would see 15 to 20 tabs open on Chrome. ☹

And that's not great because these kinds of literal "open tabs" represent at some level unfinished business, and something that I believe is contributing to some low-grade stress in my work life.

Conversely, if you were able to have let's say three to five tabs open on your Chrome internet browser, that would give you (me) a much different feeling when you wake up in the morning and logging in.

Another example of the same thing - which interestingly enough I can do well - is open word documents. Now obviously different businesses have different applications that you use on a more regular basis than others, but for me, it's Microsoft Word.

And in the past, I used to have all of these Microsoft Word tabs open. Documents I was working on, copy and paste contents I wanted to keep but hadn't renamed/saved, and it was just a lot.

But today, I've gotten myself down to 4 or 5 open Word Docs, which to be honest with you is fine because now they're the email templates/responses I use on a day-to-day basis when I'm engaging folks on social media or making introductions to people I know in my network, so that works out just fine.

But make no mistake about it: Finishing what you started is instrumental when it comes to overachieving without over-committing.

Why?

Because it gives you a sense of accomplishment.

It reduces your overall sense of overwhelm and stress.

And it does get you more focused and more successful in your business endeavors.

And if you implement some of those recommendations I think you'll find that they will also work in the fast-paced environment that we call work.

But don't take my word for it…try a couple and see for yourself!

CHAPTER 5

<u>The #1 Thing to Consistently Overachieve without Over Committing</u>

This is without a doubt, the single most important thing that I would attribute to my success when it comes to learning how to overachieve without over-committing.

Are you ready?

Letting.

Stuff.

Go.

> In other words, when I learned to be less bothered on a day-to-day basis, by challenging external circumstances, situations, and people in my life, what I found was that the overall quality of my life got better.

Things were more peaceful.

I was less upset and anxious.

And as a result, I was more successful at both home AND at work, because I spent the finite energy I did have on moving forward and making things better…versus looking backward, and being upset as to why things weren't going better.

You see as an overachiever, and I'm speaking for myself, I tended to hold on to things that happened throughout the day.

And if I'm being honest, those things were usually negative.

When I was working in corporate, it might be a disagreement I had with somebody at work, or today as a business owner, it might be a client or prospect situation that didn't go my way.

I would often find myself not only being mildly upset about it (which is perfectly reasonable), but also rehearsing that situation over and over again in my head and STAYING upset about it (less reasonable).

Now, this might not be you, but if you've ever had an argument/disagreement with someone and you find yourself going over that dialogue over and over again, thinking about what you "should have said," then that's NOT letting stuff go. ☹

Or if as an organizational professional, let's say a project you're working on doesn't achieve the desired results, and you find yourself 2 or 3 days later STILL being upset about it, again that's NOT letting go.

Or if you're at home and you and your spouse get into a slight argument, and even after you guys talk and come to some type of agreement moving forward and you're STILL resentful/upset.

(NOT letting go!).

And truth be told, it took me a while to link those two things together: Me NOT letting go of things (via my rehearsing), and feeling more stress, more anxiety, and less peace in my life.

That connection between mindset and physical and emotional well-being was never fully explained to me before, so I was having a hard time understanding why I was feeling the way I was.

But once I put 2 and 2 together, my life got better overall.

Now for the sake of clarity, I went ahead and wrote down the exact equation below.

> **Negative External Event + Me Rehearsing = Negative Mindset/Emotional Unease**

Negative Mindset / Emotional Unease + Another Quasi Negative External Event = Over Reaction AND Additional Stress AND Less Peace in my life in general

Notice that second equation: "Another quasi negative external event" which leads to an overreaction, which leads to additional stress and LESS peace in my life.

That's the part that I didn't realize until much later in life.

And I don't mind sharing that this is an area where I still struggle with on occasion today when something doesn't go as planned or the way I want it.

I have to remind myself...

Let.

It.

Go.

> If you've ever read the book, "Don't Sweat the Small Stuff," that in my mind is the conversation we're having. Most people, including myself, tend to hold onto things. But when I learned to let stuff go on at a more consistent rate, I felt myself feeling lighter and less emotional baggage throughout the day.

So with all of that in mind, what can you do to get better at letting stuff go?

Great question, and here are a couple of things I've personally done in that area.

Number 1: You have to STOP taking things so personally.

And again, this was an area I struggled with for a while. I think a lot of high achievers are like this as well, because taking things personally was a big part of how I motivated myself and moved things forward!

Tell me I can't do something at work?

Well, then I'm going to spend the next 3 days figuring out a way to get it done.

Need to get a big project done under a tight deadline?

Then I'm going to take the weekend to get it done because that's the type of person I am and the type of successful outcome I want to be associated with.

> In other words, if success was the vehicle, then "taking things personally" was the fuel by which I moved the car forward.

And truth be told, that's fine.

But as I heard my Pastor tell us one time, "Your most persistent weakness is simply your biggest strengths gone out of bounds," and that's what happens with some overachievers.

They take things so personally that when even the most minor setback takes place in their lives, they view it as a general referendum toward their self-worth.

I'm not a good worker because the project didn't work out.

I'm not a good leader because the team didn't meet its quarterly goal.

I'm not a good business owner because I'm having some challenges consistently finding new clients.

In other words, instead of viewing the negative result as a motivating force for moving forward because I want to change that outcome (a good thing), some people view it as a personal indictment regarding their ability and self-worth, causing them to double down and "prove their worth" to others.

This leads to over-the-top long hours, consistently working on the weekends, the inability to relax, and the lack of quality relations on the home front (all not great things).

Because it's no longer a result that you're looking to turn around for next time (oh, I lost this game, so I'm going to work on some things that will help me "win" next time), but instead a negative feeling about yourself that you're trying to exorcise through work.

Oh, and here's the other thing: Most things just aren't THAT important. Most people don't care or even think about what you're doing or how it makes you look.

How can I be so sure?

Because they're too busy thinking about themselves!

And I understand that as overachievers, we take great pride in our work and through extension the work product that we produce at the office. That's what has made us successful over the years.

Because we look at things and want to make them better, so to a certain extent we're always going to want to take things personally. And that's totally fine.

But just keep in mind that "you" and "the work" are two separate things.

And when the latter doesn't come out as well as you'd like, it doesn't mean something is defective with the former. Sometimes things just work out that way, and it doesn't always require us to redouble our efforts to make things right. ☺

Number 2: Focus on the process…not just the result.

When it comes to goals, we as high achievers can be VERY results-oriented. And there's nothing wrong with that. As a matter of fact, that's part of what makes us so successful in our organizations or as leaders or business owners.

But the problem is that we get so focused on the results, so focused on the numbers, that when things don't go our way we get upset at the negative result.

As opposed to not being happy with the negative result, but realizing that even though it didn't work out, we did everything we could in order to get a favorable result that just didn't happen this time.

In other words, the process we followed and the actions we took were totally fine…it just didn't yield the result we wanted.

You might be thinking, "Hold on, Brian. I did everything we could along the way but 'it just didn't work out for us and I'm supposed to be okay with that? You're really going to need to unpack that a bit please."

No problem.

Let's say I am an organizational professional who wants to get promoted by the end of next year. That promotion would be the goal and the result I want to achieve.

So a few weeks later a promotion opportunity presents itself and I'm super fired up. I type up my resume, go through the interview process, and answer all of the questions to the best of my ability…and at the end of a 3-month process, I don't get the job.

Should I be upset?

Well, the old way says absolutely!

You didn't get the job!

Of course, you should be upset!

Hilliard, you need to get your BEEEEEP in gear! What's wrong with you?

That's the old way.

Which as you're familiar with, is VERY black and white, results-oriented.

Instead, I'd like us to consider a different way. So instead of asking, "Should you be upset," how about we ask a different question: "Did you do the best you could in every step along the way to be successful?"

So with the interview, were you prepared to the point where you anticipated some questions and answered them the way you wanted?

Were you able to accentuate your strengths and highlight those results through various stories and examples?

And what about your resume…was it professionally edited and reviewed?

In short, do you feel like you gave the best possible effort THROUGHOUT THE PROCESS to be successful, but in this particular case it just didn't work out?

Because if the answer to THAT is yes, then no, you shouldn't be upset at all.

Now obviously you're not happy about the result. And yes, there are some adjustments you can make for next time. But no, just because you didn't get this job doesn't mean that all of a sudden you're not good enough or that you need to do something to prove yourself to yourself or others.

It just didn't work out.

I'm a big sports fan and I watch a lot of basketball. And I can tell you that even at the professional level, with some of the best players in the world, sometimes the ball just doesn't go in the basket, your team loses the game, and that's just how it is. It doesn't make you any less of a player or diminish your talent in any way.

Now with that said, that adverse result can motivate you to make some adjustments and play better during your next interview. Maybe you need to prepare a bit more or talk to others in the organization to get their take on what would make you more successful, or whatever the case may be.

But regardless of what you do, let's focus on the PROCESS of getting the promotion, and realize that we have to get a little better inside of that, versus thinking that you're "less than" just because you didn't hit the end goal.

And that might sound counterintuitive, especially for a high achiever because we're so focused on the results. But take my word for it: Regardless of your talent level or the people you know, things aren't always going to work out.

And how you handle that, in this case letting stuff go – and not taking things so personally, while focusing LESS on the result and more on the process – has been a literal lifesaver for me personally.

So go ahead and give it a try and during your next "not so great" outcome and see how you feel…I think you'll be surprised. ☺

CHAPTER 6

Learning to Relax

Here's another lesson I had to personally learn for myself when it comes to being more successful in life AND at work.

Learning how to relax.

People who know me are almost always surprised when I tell them that this was an area I struggled with for SEVERAL years, because today if you spend any amount of time around me, you would quickly realize that generally speaking, I'm a fairly relaxed, laid-back person.

But like I said, that was not always the case.

As a matter of fact, the main reason for all of that past stress was due to working all those hours at my corporate job. And if you've been in that situation before, you don't need me to tell you how much of a stressful environment that can be. But even after I started my own business back in 2001, I was still stressed out because I took that overall approach with me.

In other words, I took the approach that to be successful at work you had to work REALLY, REALLY (really!) hard…all the time. And if you weren't getting in early, staying late, and working like crazy in between, then you were falling behind.

And here's the confusing thing: There IS some truth to that.

So I believe that you do have to put in the effort to get the results at work. Whether you're a business leader, an organizational professional, or an entrepreneur…there is absolutely a positive correlation between "success" and "hard work."

But here's the thing that most people miss: You don't have to be working hard ALL the time to be successful.

> Or to put it differently, learning to relax IN BETWEEN all of those hard hours at work, is the key to a more balanced and successful life…both at home AND at the job.

Why?

Because everything and everyone needs a break.

Your car for example needs to have the oil changed and parts replaced.

You wouldn't leave your car on all day, every day, and expect everything to be alright for the next 10 years, would you?

Yet, that's what I see a lot of overachievers doing regularly…with predictable adverse results.

Again, I was working like crazy during the first 2 years in my business. And what did I get for my troubles?

I got sick on 3 separate occasions for 7 days each.

And when I say sick, I don't mean just a little cough or anything like that, I'm talking about being on the couch, not doing anything because my head was hurting and I was too dizzy to move.

This happened three times during a 2-year time frame.

And being a little stubborn at the time, it wasn't until the third time lying on the couch that I thought to myself, "You know, maybe what I need to do is make some changes to how I approach work. Maybe this 'always on', push, push push approach isn't the best option for me and my long term health".

And that's when it clickecd!

And for me, started the journey of what I'm now sharing on how – exactly – you can be productive at work, AND be better at relaxing in between. Because I realized that either I could give myself a break or my body could give it to me…but regardless, the current strategy of working like a crazy man wasn't working for me. ☺

So, what are some things that you can do to better, relax and move forward as it relates to having less stress and more peace in your life?

Number 1: Incorporate some type of physical activity during the regular work week.

This can be going to the gym, taking a walk, or playing basketball (which is something that I like to do a couple of times a week). But regardless, you need something that allows you to physically get out of the house/office and get into some type of situation where you are working out the stress.

And I'm not a doctor (nor do I play one on TV), but I don't think you need to be one to recognize the benefits that physical activity has on your overall emotional health and well-being.

You might be thinking, "Ok, that sounds great Brian. But how can I fit that into my busy schedule? I just don't feel like I have the time."

I can totally understand that, but here's my short answer: You have to make the time.

And I don't want to sound harsh or unsympathetic, but it's just like what I said before. You have to realize that you're either going to make the time yourself so your body can relax or your body's going to take you down and make the time for you.

It's as simple as that.

But with that said, I DO understand that you might not have several hours a day to get outside and hike or even workout. As a matter of fact, you might only have 30 to 60 mins a day, maybe 3 or 4 times a week to make this happen, and guess what?

That's fine!

Because that's the other thing about being a Type A Overachiever, we tend to think that everything has to be this "all in" or nothing type deal, and that's also not the case.

Getting in some physical activity 3 or 4 times a week (Monday through Sunday) for about 30 to 40 mins on some days, and maybe longer on others, is perfectly fine.

We're doing this to get into the habit of working the stress out of our bodies, not training for a Decathlon.

So with that said, let's take a look at some realistic ways/time frames for making this work.

If taking a walk sounds like a good first step (no pun intended), then I'd consider doing that first thing in the morning before you take a shower or get too busy with everything else.

For me, I usually get up, stretch a bit, and then I take a quick 10 to 20 min walk outside just to get the body going. You'll be surprised how calm your neighborhood is first thing in the morning.

And for me personally, I love how walks give me a chance to wake up and collect my thoughts for the day.

Now I know some of you guys might have kids and a morning walk just isn't in the cards.

No problem.

I'm going to recommend that you get your walk-in sometime during the work day (maybe at lunch) and do that 2 or 3 times during the regular work week (Mon – Fri). And if you can't do 2 or 3 times, that's fine…start with 1 and go from there.

Because that's another thing: Getting outside and walking or exercising doesn't have to be an everyday kind of thing. As I mentioned earlier, that's where we as high achievers kind of get ourselves into trouble because we think it's all or nothing, and that's just not the case.

So if your work/family situation only allows you to have 15 to 20 mins to take a walk, say 2 or 3 times a week (Mon – Fri), that's perfectly fine. As I said before, we're just trying to get into the habit of releasing that stress from our bodies, and some good physical activity is a great start.

Number 2: Get comfortable NOT working.

This was something I REALLY struggled with.

As a high performer at work, I was almost always doing or working on something work related. And it turns out that if you do something on a regular basis (say always working 5 to 6 days a week), you AND your body will get used to it…and it will become a habit.

But here's the thing: All habits aren't necessarily good ones for you.

Smoking, excessive drinking, biting your nails, endless scrolling on social media are ALL habits that aren't necessarily good ones to be doing on a regular basis.

So what I realized was I was in the habit of working, even though it might have been counterproductive to my overall health.

So it also shouldn't be too much of a surprise when I say that I had a hard time NOT doing work projects on the weekends. ☹

What would usually happen is I'd get up on Saturday, and be super busy doing a bunch of stuff for like 3 or 4 hours, checking email, finishing up a proposal, checking social media, cleaning up my office etc.. ☹

Then once I got done with all of that, I'd grab something to eat, maybe watch a show on TV, then call some friends and go out that night (it was Saturday after all). Then I'd sleep in a bit on Sunday, get up and do some "get ready for the week" kind of stuff, and by dinner time on Sunday, I'd already be thinking about what I needed to do on Monday morning! (Which usually meant not getting a great night's sleep heading into the week.)

Sound familiar?

No wonder I felt so stressed…I never really relaxed!

So here's what I'd recommend if you're feeling this way over the weekends because it has helped me out a ton!

> First, get comfortable with the fact that you don't always have to be "working" to be a contributing member of society. I know that sounds funny, but a lot of us feel that way.

Totally not true.

Secondly, find a hobby or something you like to do to fill in that non-work time on Saturdays and Sundays. This was HUGE for me because it allowed me to still move forward in my life (Dare I say "non-work life"?) while still feeling fulfilled and getting recharged.

For me, I kept it pretty easy.

In 2006 I went out and bought this new thing that allowed you to get DVDs delivered straight to your door and had a streaming element as well (I think they called it NetFlix), and watched like 2 or 3 movies a weekend!

I also made it a point to exercise more. Meaning on Saturdays, I'd spend about 30 to 60 mins working out at the gym, which REALLY helped.

During the summer, I got back into the swing of things with golf (again, no pun intended), and that was good because as anyone who's played golf knows…you don't have time to be worried about ANYTHING else when you're staring down a 4-foot putt for par.

Anyway, that meant I was spending a good bit of time on the range, working on my game, and even in the backyard as well.

I think you're getting the idea.

Pick 2 or 3 things that you like to do – but never seem to have the time to do during the week – and make it a priority to spend some time doing THOSE things over the weekend (instead of checking email), and you'll find yourself much more refreshed and ready to go come Monday. ☺

Number 3: Consider doing some meditation in the morning and/or evening before bed.

I know what you might be thinking.

"Meditation! Isn't that a little time-consuming and woo-woo all the same time?"

Short answer: No and no.

As a matter of fact, my meditation just this morning took less than 10 mins and I can even get by with 5 if I'm in a hurry.

The reason I'm such a fan of meditation is that it allows you to get centered and relaxed by calming the mind and quieting all of that inner self-talk. (By the way, a majority of most people's self-talk is negative, so simply stopping THAT for a few minutes a day is worth the effort.)

> And as far as "woo-woo" is concerned, I'll just say this: If you want to get more, you have to be more first.

In other words, if you want to get more success as a business leader, organizational professional, or entrepreneur, you have to BE more first. Which in this case entails stepping out of your comfort zone and at least being open to the idea that mindset plays a HUGE part in your everyday success

You might be thinking, "Okay Brian. I bite. What is it you're suggesting?"

Well, nothing too major. I like to do my meditations in the morning, but you can also do them at night before you go to bed or even both.

But regardless, here's what you will do:

1. Get into a quiet place where you won't be bothered.
2. Have a clear idea of what you want to say and think to yourself while you're doing it. (I'll provide an example in a second.)
3. Commit 5 mins a day for one week.

That's it.

Now about that "what do I think" part. I'm going to recommend the book, "Jewel of the Abundance" by Ellen Grace O'Brien, as I leaned on some of her work in formulating my meditation song if you will.

So here's what I say in step two.

> *I am now in the right place. I am happy, healthy, and prosperous in all ways, as I am in the constant flow of grace, abundance and blessings from God. I am loved.*

Again, there is nothing special about what I'm saying, so feel free to come up with your own. The key to meditation though is to make sure you spend the time to feel and visualize the words you're saying.

Meaning that when I say "healthy," during my meditation, I take a few seconds to envision myself jumping and playing basketball.

When I say "happy," I envision myself laughing and genuinely having a good time.

When I say "prosperous," I envision myself having the money reflective of my current business revenue target.

I think you get the idea.

Anyway, try this out at least 5 times over the next 7 days. And don't worry if your meditation bets interrupted by your thoughts. Just open your eyes, write them down on a piece of paper next to you, and jump right back into your session.

And let me tell you what, when you do even some of these things I've suggested, you will absolutely find yourself less stressed, more at peace, and probably getting a better night's sleep as well!

Go ahead and give it a try!

CHAPTER 7

<u>The Silent Saboteur for All</u>
<u>Over Achievers</u>

Now this is an area where I still personally struggle with from time to time, and truth be told, it's actually something that I just caught myself doing as I'm writing this chapter.

You might be asking, "What could THAT possibly be?"

Interrupting myself as I'm trying to get something done. ☹

Has that ever happened to you? You're focused on getting something super impactful done (let's call it a chapter for an upcoming book). And you're locked in, moving forward, then you just decide to see what's going on with email or social media or whatever the case may be!

Fast forward 10 mins later and you finally pull yourself back to the original task, only to take another 5 mins trying to remember your train of thought!

If you're like myself and others, then you're no stranger to this phenomenon.

And while there's nothing wrong with taking a much-needed break periodically, this isn't that. This is simply distracting yourself, getting derailed, and chasing the shiny object AWAY from your goal.

Needless to say, this can be a real saboteur to your day-to-day production, simply because it takes valuable time and energy away from the highly impactful things you want to get done.

> But with so many distractions out there - social media, emails, texts, phone calls - what exactly can a high achiever do to avoid interrupting themselves and getting off track?

Number 1: Turn off the notifications on your cell phone.

Yep, you heard me right…turn off the notifications on your phone.

Some of you might be thinking "What! I can't do that! How can I stay on top of all the things coming my way?"

Short answer: You'll be fine. The human race has literally existed for over 2,000 years without cell phone access or social media notifications.

The pyramids, the Great Wall, and electricity are just a few of the many innovations that happened over the years WITHOUT notifications from your phone.

Seriously, you'll be okay.

Now with that said and on a more serious note, I do understand the point, so let me share what I've done.

To begin with, I turned off the AUDIO element of my phone notifications for texts. So I still have the little bubble that comes up when I get a text telling me that I have an unread message, but I don't get the audio sound each time something comes through.

I had a friend of mine, every time he got a text it sounded like the introduction of Michael Jordan at the old Chicago Bulls stadium. (Sidebar:

Ray Clay was the announcer and those are something to hear…you should Google it.)

Anyway, let's just say it was a lot for every text!

And truth be told, you don't realize how much that will increase your focus simply by turning the audio off.

Number 2: I turned off all my notifications for social media.

So that includes both audio AND the little thought bubbles of all my social media applications because as you know, social media can be this constant, ever-present thing, so turning those off was a huge boost.

Now before full-scale panic sets in, just keep in mind that you can turn those notifications back on AFTER work, and I have no problems with that. (I think you'll find that once you realize you can get through an 8 hour work day without them on… leaving them off the next 6 hours is just fine too. But I digress.)

Personally, I leave them off entirely, and I go to social when I'm ready to… versus when a bell, buzzer, or tiny number tells me I should, but again, that's me. The point is you want to turn those bad boys off during regular work hours so that you're not tempted to go off the reservation and sabotage your success and focus in the process.

Number 3: I stopped constantly checking email, and instead made it a point to batch-process email throughout the day.

In other words, email for a lot of people has become this constant, intermediary task.

They're not too busy right now, or in between meetings or whatever, so it becomes a "let me just check my email real quick" kind of thing.

Instead, I'm recommending that you batch process your email and schedule it into your day like you would a meeting. So maybe first thing in the morning (8am) for 30 to 40 minutes, you just go through it real quick and handle the super important ones (say from your manager or team members or clients) first.

From there, maybe before lunch, you do something similar and take care of the ones you missed during your morning pass.

After that, you may come back sometime in the afternoon when you could use a little break…let's say 2:00 or 2:30pm.

And then, depending on how you feel, you do a quick little clean-up at the end of the day.

And by the way, those are just numbers you can use as a guide. So if you want to spend 20 mins or 35 to 40 as I suggested, that's fine, but I wouldn't spend more than an hour checking email at any one point in time.

The reason I like these intervals is that it allows you to stay on top of things without distracting and interrupting yourself by constantly checking them all the time.

Now something else you might be thinking is, "What if somebody emails me and they missed one of those windows?"

I hear that and I understand.

Here's what I do.

I just let people know that if they have something that is really time-sensitive, then the best way to get a hold of me is to call my cell or text. Obviously, I make sure to keep my cell with me, and that works like a charm.

(I find this technique especially successful when I'm doing presentations or traveling. And like I said earlier, I was pleasantly surprised by how open people were to a system that they could count on for immediately reaching me.)

Bottom Line: When you combine these recommendations, I think you'll find a number of things take place.

First off, the total volume of distractions will go down significantly.

Secondly, as a result, your productivity will increase precipitously.

And last but certainly not least, the overall satisfaction and success you experience at work will GREATLY increase as the stress and anxiety will DECREASE since you won't feel like you're constantly spending your time bouncing from one thing to the next.

But don't take my word for it, give it a try over the next couple of weeks and see what happens.

I think you'll be pleasantly surprised.